PROTECTING
the EARTH'S
ANIMALS

# Pollination Problems

## The Battle to Save Bees and Other Vital Animals

DIANE BAILEY

**PROTECTING the EARTH'S ANIMALS**

PROTECTING
the EARTH'S
ANIMALS

# Pollination Problems

## The Battle to Save Bees
## and
## Other Vital Animals

BY DIANE BAILEY

MC

**Mason Crest**
450 Parkway Drive, Suite D
Broomall, PA 19008
www.masoncrest.com

Series ISBN: 978-1-4222-3872-1
Hardback ISBN: 978-1-4222-3876-9
EBook ISBN: 978-1-4222-7913-7

First printing
1 3 5 7 9 8 6 4 2

Produced by Shoreline Publishing Group LLC
Santa Barbara, California
Editorial Director: James Buckley Jr.
Designer: Patty Kelley
www.shorelinepublishing.com

Library of Congress Cataloging-in-Publication Data
Names: Bailey, Diane, 1966- author.
Title: Pollination problems : the battle to save bees and other vital animals / by Diane Bailey.
Description: Broomall, PA : Mason Crest, [2017] |
Series: Protecting the Earth's animals | Includes bibliographical references and index.
Identifiers: LCCN 2017001350| ISBN 9781422238769 (hardback) | ISBN 9781422238721 (series) |
    ISBN 9781422279137 (ebook)
Subjects: LCSH: Pollination–Juvenile literature. | Pollinators–Juvenile literature. | Bees–Diseases–Juvenile literature. | Animal-plant relationships–Juvenile literature.
Classification: LCC QK926 .B325 2017 | DDC 571.8/642–dc23 LC record available at https://lccn.loc.gov/2017001350

Cover photograph by Tonny Wu/Dreamstime.com

## QR Codes disclaimer:

# CONTENTS

## KEY ICONS TO LOOK FOR

 **Words to Understand:** These words with their easy-to-understand definitions will increase the reader's understanding of the text, while building vocabulary skills.

 **Sidebars:** This boxed material within the main text allows readers to build knowledge, gain insights, explore possibilities, and broaden their perspectives by weaving together additional information to provide realistic and holistic perspectives.

 **Educational Videos:** Readers can view videos by scanning our QR codes, providing them with additional educational content to supplement the text. Examples include news coverage, moments in history, speeches, iconic moments, and much more!

 **Text-Dependent Questions:** These questions send the reader back to the text for more careful attention to the evidence presented here.

 **Research Projects:** Readers are pointed toward areas of further inquiry connected to each chapter. Suggestions are provided for projects that encourage deeper research and analysis.

**Series Glossary of Key Terms:** This back-of-the-book glossary contains terminology used throughout this series. Words found here increase the reader's ability to read and comprehend higher-level books and articles in this field.

# INTRODUCTION

**The yard at Dave Hackenberg's Pennsylvania home resembled a strange, outdoor office.** Boxes that looked like oversize filing cabinets were scattered all over. Instead of holding paper, they were filled with bees. That is, they were filled with bees until one day in 2006, when Hackenberg went out to check on them and found the boxes mostly empty. There was some food left, a few worker bees, and—the strangest part of all—the queen bee. That meant the hive had not been abandoned voluntarily. For some reason, the bees had just left and not returned.

Hackenberg was not alone. All over the country, the same thing was happening. Beekeepers reported losses in Texas and New York, California and Florida, as well as up through the Pacific Northwest and over in the Mid-Atlantic. Reports came from 27 states altogether, and that was just in the United States. There were similar reports coming in from around the world.

Hackenberg called scientists at Pennsylvania State University to tell them what was going on. The researchers then took samples of the few bees that Hackenberg still had left. What they found was disturbing: These were some sick bees.

**Why are the bees dying? Scientists are strugging to find out.**

No one knew what was going on, although there were plenty of theories. Maybe it was the use of cell phones. Maybe it was climate change. Maybe it was a Russian plot! Whatever the reason, it was bad news for bees and it was bad news for people. Bees are a type of pollinator. This means they transfer pollen from one plant to another, which is a necessary step for plants to reproduce. Without bees, hundreds of crops that people raise for food could not grow.

An apocalypse is a worldwide disaster, and it wasn't long before newspapers started calling the bee disappearances the "bee-pocalypse." Scientists scrambled to figure out what was happening. They discovered that bees are facing a host of problems, from diseases to habitat loss—and so are other insects, birds, and mammals that also pollinate plants. Fortunately, now that we understand more about what's causing the bee-pocalypse and threatening other pollinators, we can do a lot more to stop it.

## WORDS TO UNDERSTAND

**amber**   a substance formed by hardened resin, a sticky material made by trees

**dormant**   inactive

**pollinator syndrome**   the relationship between a specific type of plant and the animal that pollinates it

**ultraviolet**   a part of the light spectrum that is beyond violet and is invisible to people

# NATURE'S GRAND PLAN

**The fly-like insect called a thrip was a tiny thing, less than .08 inches (2 mm) long. When she died, it's safe to say no one paid much attention.** Just by accident, though, the thrip got a nice funeral when her body was safely preserved in a drop of **amber** until scientists found it some 105 million years later.

When the scientists examined the little thrip under a microscope, they found something interesting. Stuck to the insect's face were small, yellow grains that looked like a fine layer of dust. Those grains were pollen.

It was proof that nature had come up with the "pollination plan" tens of millions of years ago—and it still works today.

## Pass It On

Like people and animals, plants have male and female parts. To reproduce, the two have to get together. Central to this process is pollen. Pollen is a substance produced by the *anther*, or male part of a flower. For the plant to produce seeds or fruit, the pollen must be transferred to the *stigma*, the female part of the flower. This process is called pollination.

It's a simple concept, but there are actually many ways to get this job done. A few kinds of plants are self-pollinating.

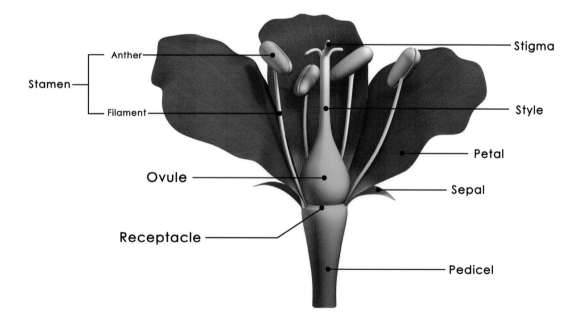

**This diagram shows a typical plant's reproductive system.**

The pollination process.

That means they can pass pollen around within a single flower, or from one flower to another on the same plant. Peas, peanuts, and sunflowers are some self-pollinating plants. Most plants rely on cross-pollination, however, and must get their pollen from a different plant of the same species.

Some plants are able to self-pollinate in a pinch, but they prefer to cross-pollinate. Cross-pollination is desirable because it produces more genetic diversity. If the members of a species are all a little different from each other, it makes the species healthier and stronger overall. Plants that have been cross-pollinated also tend to make more of whatever they make—whether it's apples or avocadoes—and the fruit is larger.

There are several things that can act as pollinators. For example, the wind can pick up pollen and blow it on to the next plant. Many grain crops, such as wheat and corn, use wind pollination. Water can also be a pollinator.

However, about three-fourths of the world's plants need dedicated animal pollinators to do the job. These include bees, butterflies, beetles, birds, bats, flies, and moths. In some places, even lizards and lemurs work as pollinators!

When an animal visits the plant looking for food, the pollen rubs up against its body and some sticks to it. Then, when the animal moves on, it transfers that pollen to the next plant.

## A Partnership

The relationship between pollinators (insects and other animals) and pollenizers (the plants that supply the pollen) is one of the most important in nature. Plants depend on pollinators to fertilize them so they can make seeds. To make sure insects and other animals stop by, plants have developed different methods to attract them.

The main way is through the use of flowers. You already know that flowers come in all shapes, sizes, smells, and colors. That makes your garden more interesting, but plants actually do not care what you think—they are much more concerned about what their pollinators think. Their flowers act like nature's billboards, designed to get animals to stop and, well, smell the flowers, so to speak.

For their part, insects and other animals don't spend time pollinating just to rack up some volunteer service. They don't even know that when they visit a plant, they're helping pollinate it. They're in it for another reason: food. Pollen itself is a good source of protein, vitamins, and min-

## SEND IN THE SPECIALISTS

Most plants make it easy for insects to find their pollen—after all, they want insects to come and visit. However, about eight percent of the world's plants are more stubborn. They make their customers work a little harder. They tuck their pollen deep inside the tube of the anther, where it's difficult to reach. That's where certain species of bees, like bumblebees, mason bees, and carpenter bees, can help. They use a special technique called *sonication*, or "buzz pollination." This means the bees quickly flex and then relax the muscles they use for flying. By "quickly," think several hundred times a second! This produces an enormous amount of force—more than what an astronaut on the space shuttle goes through. The motion creates a powerful buzz that shakes the pollen out of its tube. Tomatoes, potatoes, cranberries, blueberries, and kiwi fruit are some foods that depend on buzz pollination.

erals. Many plants also make nectar, a sugary liquid packed with energy-producing carbohydrates. To an insect, a flower is the ultimate drive-through window. These places are also great social hangouts for animals to meet potential mates and build their nests.

Timing is everything in the pollination process. Not all flowers bloom at the same time, and there's a reason for that. What if everything bloomed in the spring and nothing in the summer? Animals would have nothing to eat during the offseason. Instead, there are plants that begin blooming as soon as the cold of winter eases up, and other ones that keep it up through late fall. Most plants go **dormant** in the dead of winter, and so do most pollinators. If the weather stays warm enough through the winter, though, there are some pollinators that stay active all year long.

## Pollinator Syndromes

They may sound bad, but **pollinator syndromes** are not contagious. The term just describes how specific types of animals are matched to specific types of plants. For example, birds love bright red and pink flowers, so those are the ones they usually go for. Bees, on the other hand, can't even see the color red. However, they can see in the **ultraviolet**

**Bees get the headlines, but birds pollinate as well.**

range, which is invisible to humans. Have you ever noticed how some flowers have stripes of color leading into the center? For bees, those are like lights on a runway, leading them to the food! Bats, which work at night, like white or bluish flowers that show up better in low light.

Smell is another important factor. Bees are attracted to the pleasant scents of certain flowers. Other flowers emit odors that smell bad to humans, like rotting flesh. That's to attract certain insects who might think it's food. Birds don't have a great sense of smell, so they can pick up the slack on neutral-smelling flowers.

The shape of flowers also plays a part. Hummingbirds have long, curved beaks. As a result, they're attracted to trumpet vines, which have long, cone-shaped flowers that the hummingbirds can dive into to get nectar. (This pairing is so perfect that trumpet vine is sometimes even called hummingbird vine.) Hummingbirds hover in the air while they're eating, but butterflies need to perch somewhere. They like flowers with large, flat petals where they can rest.

An extreme case of a pollinator syndrome can be found with the Madagascar orchid and a moth called Morgan's sphinx moth. These two species are the best of friends. In fact, they each depend solely upon the other. The Madagascar orchid has an incredibly long tube, between eight and 14 inches (20 and 35 cm). The nectar is at the bottom,

**A Morgan's sphinx moth helps keep a rare orchid alive.**

so an insect must get down the tube first. The only insect up to the task is Morgan's sphinx moth. It's already a big moth, with a wingspan of about 6 inches (15.2 cm). Here's the amazing part, though: Its tongue is longer than its body is wide. The moth can reach all the way down the orchid's nectar tube. As it does, the plant's pollen rubs off on it. When the moth visits the next flower for a follow-up treat, it transfers the pollen.

## A Vital Function

The relationship between plants and pollinators goes beyond flowers and their hungry visitors. Anyone who eats plants depends on pollinators—and that's just about everyone. Plants are the major food source for most animals on the planet, including humans.

Without pollinators, you could remove a lot of food from your diet. Hundreds of vegetables, fruits, and nuts depend on pollinators. Don't like blueberries? No problem. They wouldn't be here without pollinators. Neither would cabbage and cucumbers, or peaches and pumpkins.

Or chocolate. (Remember, chocolate starts with the cocoa bean, which grows on a flowering plant that needs pollination.)

In the United States alone, it's estimated that pollinated plants are worth about $25 billion. Worldwide, roughly 75 percent of crops grown for food depend on pollinators. It's not just the food humans eat. Cattle and other livestock depend on crops like clover and alfalfa. Those also need pollinators to grow. Of course, many people depend on those animals to become food as well; without pollinated plants to eat, there would be no cows or other animals for meat.

Take a deep breath. Did you enjoy that? Thank a plant. Plants are the ones responsible for making oxygen. Humans and other animals inhale oxygen and exhale carbon dioxide. Plants do the reverse: They suck up carbon dioxide and exhale oxygen. If there were not enough plants, you wouldn't even be breathing.

Unfortunately, there is evidence that pollinators are in trouble. When you think of endangered

**If they could, cows would thank bees for helping with food.**

species, you probably picture something like rhinoceroses or whales. The smaller an animal gets, the more difficult it is to keep track of and study. However, evidence suggests that many of these species are endangered, too. Data shows that the number of bees is declining. Certain types of butterflies, birds, and bats are declining in population as well.

There are billions of these insects and animals out there, so it may seem like the planet can afford to lose a few. But they do a tremendous amount of work and each depends on the other. When things get too out of balance, it can throw off the entire system. They may be the world's littlest laborers, but without them, the planet would be very different.

## TEXT-DEPENDENT QUESTIONS

1. What part of a flower makes pollen?
2. What is one advantage of cross-pollination?
3. Why are hummingbirds good at pollinating flowers shaped like long tubes?

## RESEARCH PROJECT:

Do more research into pollinator syndromes to find out some of the combinations of plants and animals that work together.

## WORDS TO UNDERSTAND

**apiary**   a place where bees are raised

**migrate**   to travel between places according to the season

**nocturnal**   active at night

**predators**   animals that eat other animals

# A GLOBAL WORKFORCE

**It's February in central California. The temperature is 65°F (18.3°C), the sun is shining, and a slight breeze ruffles the white blossoms bursting out from the rows of almond trees.** It's pretty and perfect, so it's no surprise that visitors are arriving by the truckload.

Like, 60 billion or so visitors.

These visitors are honeybees, though, and they're not on vacation. For them, it's a business trip. Over the next few weeks, they've got a lot of work to do, pollinating the state's 900,000 acres of almonds. Almond pollination is mostly handled by European honeybees, a kind of bee that was imported from Europe during the 1600s. These honeybees are managed bees, meaning they are raised by human beekeepers in an **apiary**. Honeybees are professional pollinators, but there are also many species of wild bees that help in pollination, too.

## Experts in the Field

Bees have been around for 50 million years or so. They evolved from wasps. Wasps are **predators** that eat other insects and spiders. Bees, however, evolved to eat pollen and nectar. Basically, they are vegetarian wasps. As the bees' diet changed, so did their bodies. Wasps are smooth, but bees are covered with stiff, bristly hairs. Pollen sticks to it easily. Some species have special pouches on their legs that they can use to store and carry pollen. Physics is on their side, too. When they fly around, they build up a positive electrical charge. Flowers carry a slightly negative charge. Since opposites attract, it helps the pollen "jump" onto the bees' bodies.

Worldwide, there are about 20,000 different species of bees, with about 4,000 species in North America. Besides the well-known honeybee, there are carpenter bees and mason bees, digger bees and sweat bees, sunflower bees and blueberry bees. And don't forget the shaggy fuzzyfoot bee.

Of all the types of animals that pollinate the world's plants, bees do the most. In fact, it's estimated that for every three bites of food you eat, you can thank a bee for one of them.

Think about the different types of people you know. Do you know someone who is a hard worker? What about someone who seems to be able to do just about anything? Bees are the same way. Different species have different strengths.

Honeybees are especially important in pollination. That's a little surprising, since they are actually not that good at it. They prefer to keep most of the pollen they collect for

**The fuzz on a bee's body helps it collect the pollen from plants.**

## STAY SWEET

Bees have been an important part of human culture for thousands of years. Beeswax has been used to make candles, soap, moisturizers, and shoe polish. Honey, though, is the real prize. For a long time, it was the easiest way to satisfy a sugar craving. (Sugar itself was rare until medieval times.) It can also be used as an antibiotic, a way to fight off allergies, or a special shampoo. Since honey doesn't spoil, the ancient Egyptians even used it as an embalming fluid!

It takes a lot of bee hours to make honey. One bee only produces about one-twelfth of a teaspoon of honey in its whole life. Making honey is an involved process. First, bees suck nectar out of flowers and store it in their special "honey stomach" (not their regular stomach). After returning to their hive, they throw up the nectar and pass it along to other bees. Those bees chew on it awhile, until the nectar thickens up and becomes honey. Now it goes into the honeycomb, where it's stored until the bees need a snack—or until human beekeepers or hungry animals get at it. So, would you like some bee vomit with your toast and tea?

food, instead of depositing it on other plants. As a result, a lot of the flowers they land on do not get pollinated. Honeybees are also weather wimps. They don't like cold weather, rain, or strong winds.

**Even a bee's six legs act as collectors.**

However, they have a very important strength: numbers. A colony of honeybees may have 40,000 or 50,000 bees in it. Let them loose on an orchard of fruit trees, and they can do a tremendous amount of work in a short time. Plus, they're very orderly. Other types of bees flit around, going wherever seems interesting. Not honeybees. It's up one aisle and down the next. They also have a very long flying range. They can travel up to three miles. For growers who want to ensure that the majority of their plants get pollinated, honeybees are the answer.

Honeybees are also expert communicators. When they're out foraging for food, they take mental notes about where they are. Then, when they return to the hive, they do a special "waggle dance" to let the other bees know where the food is.

## The Bee Business

About 14 million years ago, honeybees lived in North America. At some point they became extinct on the continent, however. They were reintroduced when English settlers began arriving in America in the 1600s, and brought honeybees with them. The bees made honey, and beekeepers loaned them to area farmers to pollinate their crops.

After World War II ended in 1945, the U.S. economy began to change. Local farms began to be replaced by "big agriculture." Large corporations managed thousands of acres of crops. It was too much for native bees to handle by themselves. Beekeepers responded by raising more bees—and charging money to use them. Today, commercial beekeeping is big business. Some people keep thousands of hives, with tens of thousands of bees in each. Each year, they load their bees on trucks and take them all over the country to pollinate whatever crop needs it.

For many bees, the work starts with California's almonds. In 2016, there were roughly 90 million almond trees in the central part of the state. That's 2.5 trillion individual flowers that need pollinating. There aren't nearly enough wild pollinators to do the job, so farmers have to outsource for help. They bring in managed colonies of honeybees from

# HOW HARD CAN IT BE?

Next time you wave a fly off your brownie, consider this: Without a little fly called a midge, you wouldn't even *have* a brownie. The midge is only about .04 to .1 inches (1 to 3 mm) long, which means it can wiggle into some pretty small spaces. One of those is the flower of the cacao plant, which  provides the raw ingredient for chocolate. The cacao flower isn't wide-open and inviting, like those of many other plants. This small white flower, about the size of a dime, faces downward, and it's a bit of a maze to get inside. The midge is the only insect small enough—and determined enough—to do it. That's not even the hard part, though. Then the fly has to get back out with some pollen, and take it to the next flower. Unfortunately, these creatures can't carry much pollen with them, and they aren't very good at flying. Only a small percentage of flowers actually ends up with the pollen they need. With those odds, it's amazing the chocolate industry has survived!

faraway states such as Maine and Florida, as well as some from Australia.

After taking care of almonds, the bees might move to Michigan or Wisconsin to munch on blueberries, cranberries, or maybe some alfalfa during the spring and summer. For the fall, they can head south to Texas for some pumpkins. Unfortunately, the way the pollination business works is a lot different from how nature designed the system. When bees pollinate almonds, that's all they eat—for a month. The next month, when they move to a new crop, they eat nothing but that. Talk about a crazy diet.

## Butterflies, Birds, and Bats

When it comes down to efficiency, no pollinator beats a bee. However, they can't get the job done alone. They need a backup crew, and that's where butterflies, birds, and other animals come in. Bees stay close to home. (Even the adventurous honeybee doesn't travel more than a few miles from the hive.) Many species of birds and butterflies, however, **migrate**. They move from climate to climate depending on the season.

The monarch butterfly is one of the most recognizable species in the United States. It is about 3.5 to 4 inches

(8.9 to 10.2 cm) across, and easy to spot. The orange panes on its wings are separated by black lines and accented with white dots. Monarchs migrate long distances, traveling south from Canada and the United States to spend the winter in Mexico. Their total journey might be 3,000 miles (4,800 km). Of course, they have to eat along the way. In the process, they provide pollination services over much longer distances than bees can.

Birds are important for similar reasons. They can also travel long distances, and they can see colors that bees can't. They also stay active even in cold or rainy weather, when other insects are taking shelter. Most insects are dormant in the winter, so birds can take on the job of

**The monarch's journey is one of the longest by insects.**

pollinating flowers that bloom in the winter. Birds can also exist in climates where there aren't many insects, such as places that are dry or isolated (like islands). They can also survive in higher altitudes.

When it's bedtime for birds and bees, the bats and moths of the world are just waking up. That's when the pollination "night shift" takes over. Some flowers bloom at night, so they attract **nocturnal** animals. In eastern Africa, numerous species depend on the baobab tree. It depends on pollination mainly from bats. It blooms at night, when bats are active, and has large flowers that can support the bat's weight.

**Bees, birds . . . and bats! Flying mammals spread pollen, too.**

Talk about teamwork. Pollinators are champions when it comes to group projects. Everyone has a job, and there are no slackers. So who's getting more out of the pollination process—animals, or plants? Actually, the answer might be humans.

For more than a century, people have been steadily meddling with nature. We've changed what we grow, how much we grow, and where we grow it. Unfortunately, this approach is beginning to backfire. It does not work very well for pollinators. Without some changes, it won't work very well for us, either.

Different views of pollination.

## TEXT-DEPENDENT QUESTIONS:

1. About how many species of bees are there in the world?

2. Name one reason honeybees are good at pollinating crops.

3. What animal is the main pollinator for the baobab tree in Africa?

## RESEARCH PROJECT:

Track the journey that a honeybee takes over the course of a year. What types of crops does it pollinate in each season?

## WORDS TO UNDERSTAND

**monoculture**   a type of agriculture focused on one crop rather than many

**neonicotinoids**   a type of pesticide

**parasite**   an animal that lives on another animal's body, using it for food

# TROUBLE IN THE AIR

**How many people live in your home? You can probably count them up pretty quickly.** But try counting the number of ants. That project is a lot harder! Scientists face the same problem when they try to study small organisms such as ants or other insects. It's very difficult to figure out how many there are, and where exactly they are living. The experts do have some data, though, and it shows that the populations of many pollinators—especially bees—are shrinking.

In the United States, a survey showed that beekeepers lost almost half their bees from 2015 to 2016. The danger isn't that honeybees will go extinct anytime soon. Bees reproduce quickly, and a queen bee can lay more than 1,000 eggs a day. Beekeepers can always buy more bees, but that costs money. It may not make economic sense for them to stay in the pollination business. Also, the deaths may point to more widespread environmental problems, because it's not just managed bees that are dying. In Hawaii alone, seven species of wild bees were added to the endangered list in 2016. In 2017, the first US bumblebee species, the rusty patched bumblebee, was placed on the endangered list. It's not limited to managed bees, either. Seven species of bees in Hawaii alone are on the endangered list. Bee populations are down across the globe, from Thailand to Kenya to Chile. At least four species of

**The effects of CCD can be seen in these bee bodies in a hive.**

wild bumblebees have gone extinct in Europe. In China, so many wild bees have died that farmers have been forced to pollinate their apple trees themselves, using paintbrushes.

So what's going on?

## The Disappearing Disease

The big bee die-off was first reported in 2006, when U.S. beekeepers found that their hives were being mysteriously abandoned. It's normal for about 15 percent of managed bees to die over the winter, but these numbers were much higher than the average. Even stranger was that it did not look like a normal die-off. There were no bodies. It was as if the bees had simply wandered off and never returned.

In England, this situation was called the *Mary Celeste* syndrome, named after a ship in the 1800s that was also abandoned under unknown circumstances. The newspapers called it "Bee-pocalypse" and "Bee-mageddon," named after major disasters. Scientists, however, gave the condition a more technical name: Colony Collapse Disorder (CCD).

CCD has a distinct pattern. Although the hives are mostly abandoned, they are not completely empty. The queen bee—who runs everything—is still there. A few worker bees have stayed behind to serve her. There's also plenty of food. This means that the bees did not voluntarily move on, as they sometimes do. If that had been the case, the queen would have gone with them. They would not have left behind food supplies. Instead, most of the bees just vanished. Were they lost? Killed? Kidnapped and being held for ransom by chipmunks? No one knew.

An overview of the CCD problem.

As it turned out, CCD was not a new thing. Over the centuries, beekeepers had reported other mysterious collapses like these. This time, though, it was particularly bad, and it only got worse in the next few years. Scientists now believe that CCD isn't caused by one particular thing. It is likely a combination of factors. Bees are suffering from habitat loss, malnutrition, stress, and disease.

## Running out of Room

The problem in the United States began decades ago. After World War II, farmers began to change their agricultural practices to help feed a growing country. Instead of smaller family farms, there were huge farms run by corporations.

Backyard vegetable gardeners usually like to raise several different foods. Their goal is to put a variety of home-grown food on the table. Agricultural companies, however, are in it to make money. For them, it's more efficient and cheaper to plant large areas of a single kind of crop. This practice is known as **monoculture**. Monoculture is cost-effective, but it's terrible for pollinators. Just like people, insects, birds, and other animals need a variety of food to be healthy.

**Big agriculture has had a cumulative effect on bees.**

The rise of big agriculture had other effects on pollinators as well. With the country's growing population, companies and family farmers needed to grow more food. To create more farmland, they cut down trees and plowed up meadows. They were destroying animals' homes. Patches of clover or wildflowers became scarce, and pollinators had to travel farther and farther to find food.

Climate change may also be contributing to the problem. Over the last decades, the earth's average temperature has been steadily rising. Flowers are adjusting to the changes by blooming at different times than they have in the past.

Bees and other pollinators may not be on the same time-table anymore. They won't show up when the flowers are blooming, and by the time they get hungry, the flowers will be gone.

## Pesticides

In the past, it was common to grow a variety of different plants in a relatively small area. Each species attracted different types of insects, some of whom ate the other ones. Things were kept in balance naturally. Having more di-

**Insect-killing chemicals kill the "good" insects, too.**

versity also made plants more resistant to diseases, which could quickly spread through just one type of crop. With the rise of monoculture, farmers needed help controlling insects and weeds. They began using large amounts of artificial pesticides.

These may kill off the unwanted pests, but they also kill useful pollinators. Scientists have identified one type of insecticide that appears to be particular harmful. **Neonicotinoids** ("neonics" for short) are a widely used type of insecticide. They are similar to nicotine. The chemicals in neonics affect an insect's nervous system, causing it to act erratically.

Many growers like to use neonics because they are effective and easy to apply. They can be put directly on the soil, and a plant will soak them up through its roots. The plant is thus "vaccinated" against insects. It's also possible to coat seeds in neonics before planting them.

In high doses, neonics can quickly kill both "bad" and "good" insects—including bees. But it's the low doses that seem to be causing most of the problems. Over time, the insecticide builds up in a bee's body. The chemicals interfere with how the bee's brain works. It gets confused and loses its ability to navigate. It can get lost while out foraging. Worse, data from some studies shows that bees may actually prefer food that has neonics in it. People can get addicted to cigarettes because of the nicotine. The same thing may be happening to the bees.

At first, it was believed that neonics were much more toxic to insects than they were to mammals. However, new evidence suggests that they could be dangerous to warm-blooded animals as well. In 2014, researchers in Europe found that many native bird species were in decline. They linked it to neonics. For one thing, the neonics killed off insects that were an important part of the birds' food supply. Also, when the birds ate plants or seeds that had the chemicals in them, they were poisoned as well. Humans, who are constantly exposed to neonics in food and water, may also be affected over time.

## Invasive Species

In the 1980s, a small but dangerous threat arrived in the United States. It was a little mite named *varroa destructor*. It sounds a bit like a villain from a Harry Potter book, and it was definitely a bad guy to bees. The varroa mite was a **parasite** native to Asia, and U.S. bees did not have any natural resistance against it. The varroa hitch on to adult

## SHOW SOME SCENTS

Go outside and take a deep breath of fresh air. You may smell the scent of fresh flowers or the earthy smell that comes after a rain. But chances are you might also get a whiff of exhaust from cars, or the smoke from a nearby power plant or factory. Those are not the most pleasant odors, but they probably won't ruin your dinner. But that's exactly what's happening to bees and other pollinators. Flowers have special scent molecules that make them smell a certain way. As

the molecules float through the air, nearby pollinators can track them to find food. However, researchers at the University of Virginia have found a problem. The chemicals in the scent molecules bond with chemicals in the air pollutants. This destroys their scent. In the past, a scent molecule might be able to travel .62 miles (1 km) or so. Now, in some areas, they only get about .18 miles (.3 km) before they're put out of service. Pollinators can't smell them, and, as a result, the flowers are ignored.

honeybees and dig into their bodies. Then they suck hemo-lymph (similar to blood) from the bees. This nourishes the varroa, but weakens the bee. Worse, when the bees return to their hives, the mites then latch onto the larva of young bees. Although the varroa mite is about the size of the head of a pin, that's pretty big to a bee. Imagine if you had an eight-legged hungry bug the size of a dinner plate stuck on your back!

The varroa mite can transmit a number of viruses that are deadly to bees. Some of these diseases cause bees to have deformed wings. Or they may become paralyzed and unable to fly. The viruses can spread quickly throughout a

**Is this the villain? The varroa mite might be killing bees, too.**

colony. Eventually they can kill off most of the bees.

Invasive species can affect pollination in other ways, too. When non-native plant species are brought into an area, they can also serve as a distraction to the area's native pollinators. Bees, butterflies, or other animals will start visiting the flowers of those plants, rather than the ones they're supposed to be eating.

A lot of things are working against pollinators. To make things better, however, people are starting to do some things that will work in their favor.

## TEXT-DEPENDENT QUESTIONS

1. How have farmers in China pollinated trees when there were not enough bees to do it?

2. What is one way American farming practices hurt pollinators?

3. What common drug are neonicotinoids similar to?

## RESEARCH PROJECT

Find out more about Colony Collapse Disorder, and how the things that cause it are interrelated.

## WORDS TO UNDERSTAND

**hybrid**   a combination of two or more things, often artificial

**invertebrate**   an animal that has no spine

**task force**   a group of people assigned to a specific project

# TACKLING THE PROBLEM

**"What are we doing on bees?" That's what President Barack Obama asked his White House science adviser back in 2013.** "Are we doing enough?" The president knew that bees were in trouble. He wanted to make sure the government was doing something about it.

## Going Global

By 2014 the White House had formed a **task force** to look into the problem. In 2015, a national strategy came out for helping the country's bees and other pollinators. There were three main goals: stop the decline of honeybees, increase the number of monarch butterflies, and improve 7 million acres of pollinators' natural habitat. To get the job done, government agencies and private organizations are working together to increase habitat and manage lands, decrease the use of pesticides, encourage scientific research, and raise public awareness.

**People have been trying to help traveling pollinators.**

Bees don't have passports, of course. They don't care about international boundaries. Solving the problem will require countries all over the world to work to save pollinators. In 2012, the European Union took a big step by outlawing the use of neonicotinoids. That hasn't happened in the United States, but environmental groups have pressured the Environmental Protection Agency (EPA) to take a closer look at them. Meanwhile, organizations in the United States,

Europe, and Mexico are working to establish more natural land for bees and other pollinators. There are also organizations that teach beekeeping to people in less developed countries. This gives them a business to help them make money, and also improves the bee populations.

## Highways and Hotels

It's all about habitat. The Xerces Society is a nonprofit organization focused on protecting **invertebrate** species like insects. From 2015 to 2016, the organization helped add about 150,000 acres nationwide to be attractive to pollinators. For example, they worked with California almond growers to plant shrubs and wildflowers among the almond groves, to help attract native pollinators. They're also working with state governments to plant flowers along the millions of miles of roads stretched across the country. These are especially important because they can connect pollinators to different areas.

The monarch butterfly is a good example. Each year these butterflies fly south to spend the winter in Mexico, then back north to the U.S. and Canada for the spring and summer. The loss of habitat and food sources along the way has made this trip harder and harder for the monarchs.

US plans to help monarchs.

Worse, the monarch caterpillars are picky eaters. They only eat one thing, a certain species of a plant called milkweed. Milkweed has died out because of pesticide use, so there's not as much for the caterpillars. From 1990 to 2015, the population of monarchs shrank by almost a billion butterflies. There were only about 30 million left.

In 2014, the governments of the United States, Mexico, and Canada pledged to work together to help the monarch. In Mexico, the government is working to stop logging that destroys the habitat where monarchs spend the winter. Farther north, citizens in the U.S. and Canada are being encouraged to plant milkweed or other plants for monarchs. In the U.S., it's common for cars, bicycles, and pedestrians to share the road. Now we can count monarchs among the travelers. As of 2016, they have an official "monarch highway." The I-35 interstate runs north and south from Minnesota into Texas. The governments of all six states that the highway goes through have agreed to plant pollinator habitats along the side of the road to help the monarch.

There are already results. In the mid-1990s, the monarchs occupied about 44 acres (17 hectares) in Mexico

**A thriving monarch grove can contains thousands of insects.**

during the winter. By 2013, that number had shrunk to just over an acre and a half (0.6 hectares), or about the size of a football field. But the efforts to increase their habitat are paying off. By the winter of 2016, they'd rebounded to winter over about 10 acres (4 hectares).

Bees don't travel nearly as far as monarchs, but they need a place to rest their weary bodies, too. In lots of places, they can check in at a special "bee hotel." Scientists from the University of New Hampshire built a hotel out of bricks, sticks, rocks and cement blocks. The materials all have little holes in them, providing cozy rooms for the bees. The idea behind the hotel was to attract the region's native bees, so that researchers could study them. A Girl Scout

# PLANT A POLLINATOR GARDEN

Are you one in a million? People involved with the National Pollinator Garden Network hope so. The group works to increase pollinator habitats, and has set a goal of getting 1,000,000 new pollinator gardens planted nationwide. It doesn't have to be huge—even a window-box garden will help. Here are some tips for creating a successful pollinator garden.

**Choose Your Space.** Pick a spot that's sunny and is protected from too much wind.

**Go Native.** You may like to try exotic foods, but pollinators are less adventurous. Find out what plants grow naturally in your region. Insects have evolved to get what they need from these native plants. (There are lots of websites with this information.) Also, avoid **hybrid** plants with double blooms—they often don't have the pollen that insects need.

**Plan Ahead.** Choose flowers that bloom at a variety of times throughout the year. Ideally, you'll want some things that come up at the beginning of spring, to get things rolling, and then others that last through the summer and into the fall.

**Think Big.** Planting snapdragons among the sunflowers may appeal to you, but it's not the best arrangement for pollinators. If you have enough room, focus on "advertising" your garden by planting a larger area of a single species, and then moving on to the next one, rather than mixing them together.

**Keep it Clean.** Avoid using pesticides and herbicides. These can be very harmful to insects and other animals that visit your garden. Pull weeds by hand, and don't worry about insects nibbling holes in a few leaves. Remember, your garden doesn't have to look perfect—it's much better if it's healthy.

**Make a Whole Habitat.** Flowers are just one part of a pollinator's habitat. Consider adding a water source to keep your tiny friends from getting thirsty. A salt lick provides extra nutrients. (Sea salt is better than regular salt.) Butterflies and other insects also appreciate other food, like overripe fruit. Leave dead branches and leaves on the ground to provide nesting places.

**When you finish, visit www.millionpollinatorgardens. org to find out how to register your garden.**

troop in Kansas helped build a bee hotel using hollow bamboo poles and even tubes of rolled-up paper. The hotel has room for more than 3,000 area bees. There are more hotels all over the world. The hotels do have a few problems: wasps are also attracted to them (especially if they are in the shade). If they're too tall, the bees won't fly up to them. However, if they are built properly, they can provide some extra habitat.

## City Bees, Country Bees

You'd expect to find bees in a grassy meadow or even your backyard garden. But what about the roof of a fancy hotel in New York? Twenty stories in the air, on a rooftop deck at the Waldorf-Astoria, live six hives of bees—about 300,000 of them. They've got a great view of the city's famous Central Park, where they go to feed. The bees are doing their part to help pollinate the city's flowers. Meanwhile, the hotel's chefs use the bees' honey in the hotel's restaurants.

Urban beekeeping is not widespread, especially in the United States. In fact, in New York, it was illegal until 2010. Few people wanted their neighbors hosting thousands of potential stingers. Beekeeping was declared illegal in the

## ROBOBEE

It flies! It dives! It swims and hovers. It's not actually alive, but the researchers at Harvard University created a RoboBee that acts like it. RoboBee was created based on the three B's of a bee's biology: body, brain, and behavior. It's roughly the size of a penny—but with legs and wings that stick out. Researchers have solved some of the technical difficulties of getting such a tiny thing to fly, although they're still working on getting the RoboBees to communicate with each other. RoboBees were created to be used in the military for search-and-rescue missions. Another possibility is to use them as artificial pollinators. However, researchers point out that the technology to do that is still 20 years in the future. Even then, they will only be part of the solution.

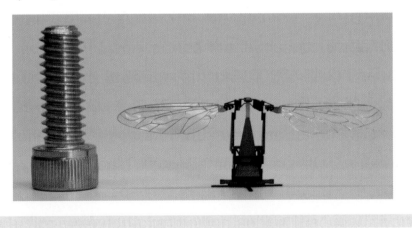

city of Los Angeles about 150 years ago, when people noticed that bees loved fruit trees and assumed that the bees were damaging the trees. Obviously, that turned out to be nonsense, but the law stayed on the books until 2015.

Can urban beekeepers really do anything to help the bee situation? As more and more land is developed into towns and cities, "city bees" have a part to play as much as "country bees." Most people who live in urban areas and keep bees have small operations, with less than 10 colonies. That won't make much of a dent in the industry of commercial pollination. However, these smaller colonies can help fill in the gaps in local communities.

## Branching Out

The millions of honeybees in America—and around the world—do a tremendous amount of pollinating. A big reason for that is that people keep "hiring" the same workers. But that doesn't mean that other workers can't chip in, too. Other species of bees can pick up the slack—or even do some of the heavy lifting. Mason bees, for example, are very efficient pollinators, and they're easy to raise. Wild bees such as bumblebees can help out if they have more habitat. There's also evidence that when wild bees are sharing an environment with honeybees, the honeybees get better at their jobs.

The honeybee we're familiar with came from Europe, but honeybees also live in Africa. Back in the 1950s, scientists in Brazil decided to bring some African honeybees to South America. They wanted to see if they could live in the tropical climate better than the European bees. Someone accidentally released the bees from their hives, however. Before long these bees had mated with European honeybees, and the Africanized honeybee was born. It wouldn't seem like such a big deal, except that African honeybees behave much differently than their European relatives. They get annoyed much more quickly, and they're not afraid to attack in large numbers. It wasn't long before these bees got a bad

**They're busy now, but watch out for Africanized honeybees.**

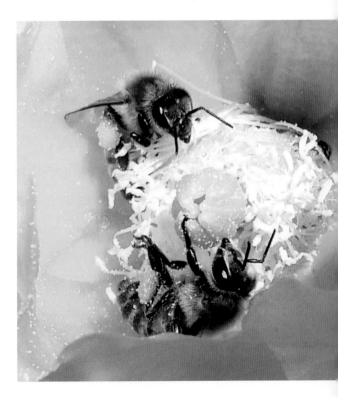

**Beekeepers will play a big role in helping bees recover.**

name: killer bees. (In truth, very few people have died from killer bee attacks.)

However, Africanized honeybees are great pollinators, just like European honeybees. Scientists have also discovered that they are more resistant to certain pests, like the varroa mite. Beekeepers in warmer climates, such as countries in South and Central America, have started using Africanized honeybees as pollinators. They require treatment that is a little different from the gentle European honeybee, but can still be raised.

Diversity is key to the survival of an ecosystem. It was a

milestone in the earth's history when plants and pollinators evolved to depend on each other, but it can't be just a one-way street. The people who depend on these pollinators have to make sure they are protected and can do their vital jobs.

## TEXT-DEPENDENT QUESTIONS

1. Where have neonicotinoids been outlawed?

2. What plant do monarch larvae eat?

3. Besides European honeybees, what is another species of bee that people can raise to be pollinators?

## RESEARCH PROJECT

Research how to build a bee hotel. What materials do you need? Where should it be placed?

**Be Lazy.** A perfectly mowed lawn with no weeds may look nice to people, but it's a disaster for pollinators. It's as if you went to the grocery store and the shelves had nothing on them. An easy way to increase habitat for pollinators is to leave at least part of your yard in a more natural state. This gives polllinators more varied food sources, and places to build their nests.

**S.H.A.R.E.** Through the Pollinator Partnership, anyone can plant a pollinator-friendly garden. The group's S.H.A.R.E. (Simply Have Areas Reserved for the Environment) program offers tips on what to plant, and you can then register it on the site. The garden does not have to be large or elaborate—if enough people do it, a little can go a long way.

**Go Organic.** Organic foods are ones that have not been treated with herbicides or pesticides to make them grow bigger and faster and protect them from pests. They usually cost more because they are a little harder to grow. However, it's also much more likely that these foods are helping attract native pollinators.

**Keep Your Eyes Open.** Keeping track of pollinators requires the efforts of a lot of people. Be a "citizen scientist" and help the professionals by recording—and reporting—what's happening in your own backyard. There are programs in many states that rely on regular people to count monarch butterflies, bumblebees, and other pollinators, or to observe their habits. A good place to start is with The Great Sunflower Project (www.greatsunflower.org).

**Spread the Word.** Check out the websites of places like the Xerces Society, the Pollinator Partnership, and the U.S. Forest Service to find out how pollinators are doing overall, and what's being done to help them. You can sign petitions and let government representatives know that you care about what happens to pollinators. Then, make sure you let others know.

# FIND OUT MORE

## BOOKS:

Angel, Heather. *Pollination Power.* Chicago: University of Chicago Press, 2016.

Burns, Loree Griffin. *The Hive Detectives*. New York: Houghton Mifflin Books for Children, 2010.

*Gardening for Birds, Butterflies, and Bees: Everything You Need to Know to Create a Wildlife Habitat in Your Backyard.* Pleasantville, NY: Reader's Digest, 2016.

Markle, Sandra. *The Case of the Vanishing Honeybees.* Minneapolis: Millbrook Press, 2013.

Pasternak, Carol. *How to Raise Monarch Butterflies: A Step-by-Step Guide for Kids.* Toronto: Firefly Books, 2012.

## WEBSITES:

**www.pollinator.org**
The Pollinator Partnership brings together several organizations that work to help pollinator species and habitats.

**www.fs.fed.us/wildflowers/pollinators/**
Check out this section on the website for the U.S. Forest Service to find out more about how pollination works, and what kinds of pollinators live in different regions of the United States.

**www.xerces.org/pollinator-conservation/**
The Xerces Society—named after an extinct butterfly—works to protect invertebrate species and is actively involved with saving pollinators.

# SERIES GLOSSARY OF KEY TERMS

**acidification**  the process of making something have a higher acid concentration, a process happening now to world oceans

**activist**  someone who works for a particular cause or issue

**biodiverse**  having a large variety of plants and animals in a particular area

**ecosystem**  the places where many species live, and how they interact with each other and their environment

**habitat**  the type of area a particular type of animal typically lives in, with a common landscape, climate, and food sources

**keystone**  a part of a system that everything else depends on

**poaching**  illegally killing protected or privately-owned animals

**pollination**  the process of fertilizing plants, often accomplished by transferring pollen from plant to plant

**sustain**  to keep up something over a long period of time

**toxin**  a poison

# INDEX

# PHOTO CREDITS

Adobe Images: Trish23 6, uduhunt 20, chanelle 22, Anotolili 25, Kletr 27, Heinz Waldacut 34, Ludmila Smite 37, lakephotography 48, Sarayuth3390 52, Cheri133 58, Wavebreakmicromedia 60, Syda Productions 61. Alamy: Natural History Museum London 18. Dreamstime.com: Sate33 8, Likrista82 10, 7activestudio 12, Meisterphoto 15, Angeldibilio 17, Jelena Gorlats 29, Pimmimemom 31, Petro Petruskyy 35, Satita Srihin 38, Shannon Fagan 41, Verastuchelova 42, Rinus Baak 51, Gunold 53. Eliza Grinnell/Harvard: 55. US Forest Service: 46. MartinTuttle. org: 32. .

# ABOUT THE AUTHOR

**Diane Bailey** has written dozens of nonfiction books for kids and teens, on topics ranging from sports to science. She has two sons and lives in Kansas.